# NATURAL DISASTERS!

COSTUME PARTY

Johannah Haney
Illustrated by Tom Casteel

# Titles in the **Explore Earth Science** Set

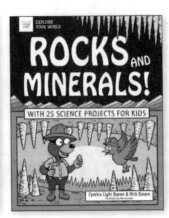
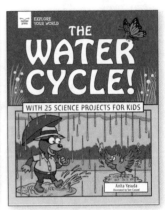

Check out more titles at www.nomadpress.net

Nomad Press

A division of Nomad Communications

10 9 8 7 6 5 4 3 2 1

This book was manufactured by Versa Press, East Peoria, Illinois
February 2020, Job #J19-11233
ISBN Softcover: 978-1-61930-862-6
ISBN Hardcover: 978-1-61930-859-6

Educational Consultant, Marla Conn

Questions regarding the ordering of this book should be addressed to
Nomad Press
2456 Christian St., White River Junction, VT 05001
www.nomadpress.net

Printed in the United States.

# CONTENTS

**Interested in primary sources? Look for this icon.** Use a smartphone or tablet app to scan the QR code and explore more! Photos are also primary sources because a photograph takes a picture at the moment something happens.

You can find a list of URLs on the Resources page. If the QR code doesn't work, try searching the internet with the Keyword Prompts to find other helpful sources.

→ 🔍 EXPLORE NATURAL DISASTERS

## BLIZZARDS

The first blizzard to be declared a federal emergency was in upstate New York and southern Ohio in 1977.

## VOLCANOES

There are around 1,300 active volcanoes in the world today, but only 20 or 30 erupt each year.

## WILDFIRES

The United States spends billions of dollars every year fighting wildfires.

## HURRICANES

Hurricanes create violent winds, heavy rain, high waves, widespread flooding, and even tornadoes.

## TORNADOES

The United States has an average of 1,200 tornadoes every year, more than any other country.

## TSUNAMIS

Tsunamis can travel across entire oceans and lose little energy as they move.

## INTRODUCTION

# WHAT IS A NATURAL DISASTER?

**Imagine you live in the midwestern United States and the sky takes on a strange greenish color in the middle of a summer day. Suddenly, a tornado warning is issued and everyone scrambles for cover in basements and bathrooms.**

Tornadoes are a fact of life in many parts of the United States each year. Or maybe you live on the East Coast of the United States and you hear news that a hurricane is bearing down on your area in the next couple days.

**WORDS ⊚ KNOW**

**tornado:** a swirling vortex of wind in a funnel shape that extends toward the earth from a large storm system.

**hurricane:** a powerful storm with winds of at least 74 miles per hour.

1

# NATURAL DISASTERS!

Or maybe you live on the West Coast of the United States, where an earthquake could shake the ground at any moment.

Natural disasters are events that occur in nature that cause widespread destruction of lives and property. These natural events have incredible power, and can be pretty awe-inspiring to think about or watch. During natural disasters, people are hurt or even killed, homes and farms destroyed, and livestock lost.

Natural disasters can happen anywhere, but certain areas are more likely to be the sites of specific natural disasters.

THE ERUPTION OF MOUNT PINATUBO IN THE PHILIPPINES, 1991
CREDIT: DAVE HARLOW, USGS

For example, California is at risk for large earthquakes. While small earthquakes can happen all around the United States, usually only sensitive instruments can detect them. Most cause no problems for people. But California has had many large earthquakes that brought human activity to a halt.

Another example is volcanoes—a volcano will almost certainly not erupt in the flat state of Ohio, at least not in your lifetime or during the lifetimes of your kids, grandkids, and great-grandkids! But if you live in Hawaii, that is a different story.

**volcano:** a mountain formed by magma or ash forcing its way from deep inside the earth to the surface.

**tectonic plates:** large sections of the earth's crust that move on top of the hot, melted layer below.

**eruption:** a violent explosion of gas, steam, magma, or ash.

**magma:** molten rock within the layer of earth just below the earth's crust.

**lava:** magma that has risen to the surface of the earth.

**WORDS ⊕ KNOW**

## TYPES OF DISASTERS

Not all areas of the world experience the same kinds of natural disasters. Earthquakes, which are a sudden, strong shaking of the ground, occur in areas where tectonic plates shift. Volcanic eruptions occur when molten magma comes to the surface of the earth's crust through a volcano and flows out as lava.

### DID YOU KNOW?

The state of Hawaii has five active volcanoes. One of them, named Kilauea, has been erupting for 35 years, since 1983. Another, Loihi, is underwater and has been erupting since 1996. As its lava flows build it up, Loihi may eventually break the surface of the water and become a new Hawaiian island.

3

**storm surge:** high sea levels that can occur after a big storm, such as a hurricane.

**precipitation:** fresh water that falls from clouds in the form of rain, ice, snow, hail, mist, or sleet.

**flood:** when water covers an area that is usually dry, an event caused by rain, a collapsed dam, or rising sea levels.

**drought:** a long period without rain, leading to dry conditions and a scarcity of fresh water.

**waterspout:** a tornado that occurs over water.

**wildfire:** a fire that spreads quickly, usually across a large area of land.

## WORDS TO KNOW

## LOOK FOR THE HELPERS

Beloved children's television host Mister Fred Rogers once said, "When I was a boy and I would see scary things in the news, my mother would say to me, 'Look for the helpers. You will always find people who are helping.' To this day, especially in times of 'disaster,' I remember my mother's words, and I am always comforted by realizing that there are still so many helpers—so many caring people in this world."

Hurricanes swirl toward coastlines and are capable of lots of damage to property, both through wind and storm surge. These intense storms are dangerous to life as well.

Even something as common as precipitation can result in a natural disaster! Too much rain is one cause of floods, and not enough rain causes drought. Ice storms and blizzards both can be dangerous to lives and people's homes. Tornadoes, whether they occur with hurricanes or just on their own, and waterspouts are also natural disasters. Wildfires can destroy huge areas of land, including entire neighborhoods. Fire also puts lives in danger.

You can watch one of the first videos made after a natural storm, filmed by Thomas Edison in 1900!

🔎 GALVESTON STORM VIDEO

## SCARY STUFF!

Do all these disasters sound scary to you? Well, the truth is that all of these disasters truly are scary for those living through them. If you learn about natural disasters, work to be prepared, and understand what to do during and after natural disasters, you can control your own safety.

There are many people who work hard to help before, during, and after natural disasters. Firefighters and rescue teams help take control of situations that are immediately dangerous. Doctors and nurses take care of people who may be hurt.

AFTER A HURRICANE HIT HAITI IN 2016, U.S. MILITARY FORCES WERE SENT TO HELP.
CREDIT: U.S. AIR FORCE PHOTO BY STAFF SGT. PAUL LABBE

When disasters happen, people from around the world pull together. They raise money and bring supplies to areas in trouble.

Sometimes, all it takes to help take some of the fear away is an understanding about how these natural disasters work. What factors go into a natural disaster? What makes them worse? What can make them better? How can we prepare for the kinds of natural disasters that happen in our area?

In this book, we'll take a look at the different types of natural disasters and discover the science behind them, while also learning ways to protect ourselves during an actual event. You'll learn about earthquakes, volcanoes, floods and droughts, wildfires, tornadoes, and hurricanes and typhoons. Ready to dive into the amazing world of natural disasters? Let's go!

# GOOD SCIENCE PRACTICES

Every good scientist keeps a science journal! Choose a notebook to use as your science journal. Write down your ideas, observations, and comparisons as you read this book.

For each project in this book, make and use a scientific method worksheet, like the one shown here. Scientists use the scientific method to keep their experiments organized. A scientific method worksheet will help you keep track of your observations and results.

Each chapter of this book begins with a question to help guide your exploration of natural disasters.

## Scientific Method Worksheet

**Question:** What are we trying to find out? What problem are we trying to solve?

**Research:** What information is already known?

**Hypothesis/Prediction:** What do I think the answer will be?

**Equipment:** What supplies do I need?

**Method:** What steps will I follow?

**Results:** What happened? Why?

### INVESTIGATE!

What kinds of natural disasters are common where you live?

Keep the question in your mind as you read the chapter. Record your thoughts, questions, and observations in your science journal. At the end of each chapter, use your science journal to record your thoughts and answers. Does your answer change as you read the chapter?

# PROJECT!

## PREPARE FOR A NATURAL DISASTER

**One way to stay safe in a natural disaster is to make a plan before disaster strikes. In this activity, you will make a concrete plan for natural disasters that might happen in your area.**

**1** Research natural disasters that could happen in your area. Maybe ideas will come to your mind right away. With an adult's permission, head to the library or use the internet to find out which natural disasters might happen where you live.

**2** Make an emergency plan. Working on your own, with a small group of classmates, or with family members, think about what kinds of things will keep you safe during and just after a natural disaster.

- Will you know in advance if a natural disaster is approaching? If so, how much notice will you have?

- What preparations do you need to do just before? For example, if you live in an area of hurricanes and you have some notice, you might be able to put wood shutters over the windows of your home.

- What supplies will you need? Should you get them just before a natural disaster or should you make an emergency supply kit well before you even know there is going to be a natural disaster in your area?

- Where should you go before, during, and after the natural disaster? How will you get there?

- After the immediate threat of the natural disaster has passed, are there still dangers to be on the lookout for? What might those be? How can you stay safe?

# PROJECT!

**TRY THIS!** Pack an emergency kit for your home! What might you need in case of a natural disaster? Do some research and gather items in a container to keep them safe. Make sure everyone in your house knows where the kit is.

### Here are some ideas for an emergency preparedness kit! What else might you add to it?

| | |
|---|---|
| Water—one gallon of water per person per day for at least three days, for drinking and sanitation | Cell phone with chargers and a backup battery |
| Food—a three-day supply of non-perishable food | Prescription medications |
| Manual can opener | Non-prescription medications |
| Battery-powered radio | Pet food and extra water for your pet |
| Extra batteries | Important family documents |
| Flashlights | Sleeping bag or warm blanket for each person |
| First aid kit | Complete change of clothing and comfortable shoes |
| Garbage bags | Matches in a waterproof container |
| Toilet paper and wipes | Books, games, and puzzles |
| Local maps | Stuffed animals |

## CHAPTER 1

# EARTHQUAKES AND TSUNAMIS

On April 18, 1906, residents of San Francisco, California, woke at dawn to the sound of deep rumbling coming from the ground. The earth was shaking! Soon, the sounds of church bells rang through the city. The churches were swaying back and forth with the ground, causing the bells to move and ring.

Back then, houses and schools and offices in San Francisco weren't built to withstand a big earthquake—many of them crumbled and collapsed. The earthquake also damaged the water pipes that supplied the fire departments with water.

**? INVESTIGATE!**

What are some dangers of earthquakes?

Gas pipes were also damaged, which started many fires. In the three days after the earthquake, fires across the city consumed rubble and even buildings that had survived the earthquake itself.

Firefighters had very few ways to fight the flames. Regular citizens struggled alongside firefighters to control the fires any way they could. Some used water they had in their homes to try to prevent the flames from spreading. Others used thick blankets and even clothing to tamp down smaller flames.

In the meantime, people tried to leave the city by taking ferry boats across the bay to Oakland. Others set up tents or simply slept on the grass in Golden Gate Park, where they felt safer from the aftershocks that were rolling underground. Sleeping in the open was a way to avoid the fires, too.

A STATUE THAT FELL FROM A BUILDING DURING THE 1906 EARTHQUAKE

**adapt:** to change in order to survive.

**Pangaea:** a supercontinent that existed about 300 million years ago. It contained all the land on the earth.

About 3,000 people died in the San Francisco earthquake and fires, and more than 80 percent of the city was destroyed.

In the years since this earthquake, people have come up with designs for buildings that keep people as safe as possible. It's one way humans have adapted to the world!

What caused this San Francisco earthquake? To answer that, we must travel really far back in time!

## PANGAEA

Let's look at the landmasses that make up the different continents: South America, North America, Africa, Asia, Europe, Antarctica, and Australia. These continents were not always located where they are today. In fact, the continents continue to move a little bit every year!

Scientists believe that long, long ago, the earth had one landmass that included almost all the continents we know today. Scientists named this giant landmass Pangaea.

Around 200 million years ago, Pangaea began to break apart into separate landmasses. During hundreds of millions of years, they moved apart from each other and ended up where they are today.

HOW DO YOU CUT THE SEA IN HALF?

With a see-saw!

But . . . they're still moving! Not fast enough that we feel it, but every year, the continents move about 1 inch. That's about as fast as your fingernails grow.

What makes the continents move? Let's talk about plates—tectonic plates!

## TECTONIC PLATES

The earth has three main layers—the core, the mantle, and the crust. The core is the deepest layer and is extremely hot. It has two parts, an inner core and an outer core. The inner core is solid. Scientists believe it's made of nickel and iron, but it's too deep for anyone to get a sample. The outer core is also made of nickel and iron, but this layer is liquid.

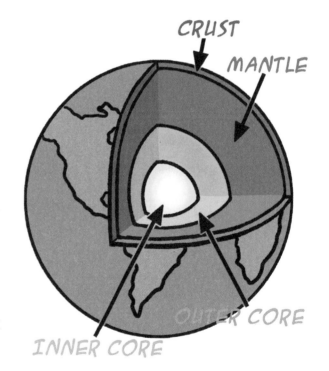

The mantle is made of very hot rock, but the closer it is to the crust, the cooler it gets.

The outer layer of the earth is the crust. The crust and the upper part of the mantle are broken into huge pieces called tectonic plates. These plates are continuously moving, very slowly, over the molten rock of the mantle.

The U. S. Geologic Survey is the government agency that studies earthquakes. You can use its interactive tools to explore earthquakes. **Use this one to see where earthquakes have recently occurred.**

🔎 USGS EARTHQUAKE CATALOG

What does this have to do with earthquakes? The place where two plates meet each other is called a boundary. And boundaries are made up of faults. A fault is a crack in the earth's surface. In an active fault, rock edges grind and scrape together, building up pressure. If the rock edges suddenly slip past one another, that pressure is released, and it causes the ground to move, sometimes violently. This is an earthquake!

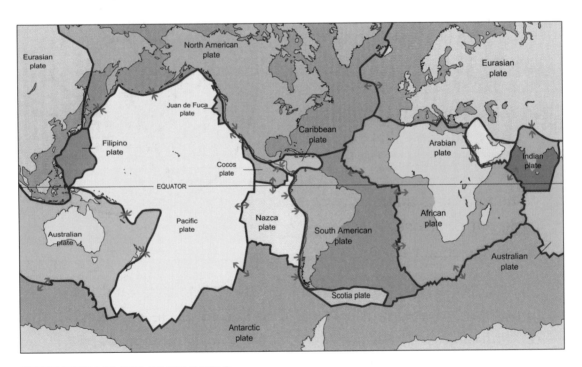

THE TECTONIC PLATES OF THE WORLD

## DID YOU KNOW?

The San Andreas fault is a famous fault running 750 miles through California. It is at the tectonic boundary between the Pacific Plate and the North American Plate.

**WORDS TO KNOW**

**tsunami:** an enormous wave formed by a disturbance under the water, such as an earthquake or a volcano.

**Richter scale:** a scale that was used to measure the strength of an earthquake.

**moment magnitude scale:** a scale that scientists use to measure an earthquake's size and strength.

## TSUNAMIS!

Imagine you're standing still in a swimming pool. If you hold your hand a couple of inches under the water, then make a sudden movement with your hand, what happens to the still water in the pool? Waves!

The same thing happens when an earthquake takes place under the sea floor, but the waves are much, much bigger. Tsunamis usually form when an earthquake happens underwater, and a large amount of water is suddenly moved. That creates a wave that travels very quickly and very far. Out in deep water, there's plenty of space for all that water, and a tsunami might not even be noticed. But if that wave meets with land, the water can gush very far onto shore, sometimes miles inland, wrecking everything in its path.

## MEASURING EARTHQUAKES

You might hear an earthquake described with a number. For example, a news reporter might say an earthquake measured a magnitude of 7.0. This number indicates how strong the earthquake was. The scale that used to be used was called the Richter scale. It was invented by a man named Charles F. Richter (1900–1985) in 1934. Scientists now use a more accurate scale called the moment magnitude scale.

# NATURAL DISASTERS!

In 2004, this is what happened in India. An earthquake off the coast of Sumatra registered a magnitude of 9.1. Several hours later, the coasts around the Indian Ocean were hit with a series of giant waves—some reached heights of 100 feet as they traveled inland. Hundreds of thousands of people died and many buildings were destroyed.

A VILLAGE IN SUMATRA AFTER THE 2004 TSUNAMI
CREDIT: U.S. NAVY PHOTO BY PHOTOGRAPHER'S MATE 2ND CLASS PHILIP A. MCDANIEL

## STAYING SAFE IN EARTHQUAKES

Many places around the world now have warning systems so that the public is alerted if signs point toward an earthquake. And in cities that are built on faults where earthquakes are more likely, engineers design buildings that can withstand the moving and shaking without getting damaged.

Wherever you live, some simple planning ahead of time with your family is a great way to stay safe in case of any natural disaster. Here are some tips.

✳ Create an emergency box with some nonperishable food items, a radio, extra batteries, a first aid kit, flashlights, and water.

✳ Plan an evacuation route from your home and arrange a meeting point somewhere in your neighborhood.

✳ Make sure there are fire extinguishers in your house and ask an adult to keep them up to date.

✳ Keep large or heavy objects on lower shelves.

✳ Ask an adult to place heavy items such as paintings or mirrors away from beds or seating areas.

✳ If an earthquake happens, stay inside.

✳ Keep away from heavy objects that might fall, such as bookcases.

✳ Stay under a desk or table until the shaking stops.

Earthquakes are rare, and earthquakes that happen where people live are even rarer. Even so, it's always good to be prepared! In the next chapter, we'll learn about a different kind of natural disaster—volcanoes! Boom!

**? CONSIDER AND DISCUSS**

**It's time to consider and discuss:** What are some dangers of earthquakes?

# PROJECT!

## MAKE A SHAKE TABLE

**One way engineers develop new ways of constructing earthquake-safe buildings is by testing models on a shake table. Build your own!**

**1** Place the two pieces of cardboard against each other and wrap the elastic bands around them, spreading the bands apart from each other.

**2** Carefully slip the tennis balls between the pieces of cardboard. Space the balls evenly near the corners.

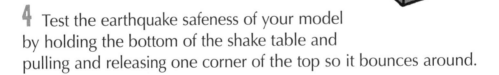

**3** Build a model home out of Legos, popsicle sticks, or some other material. Place it on top of your shake table.

**4** Test the earthquake safeness of your model by holding the bottom of the shake table and pulling and releasing one corner of the top so it bounces around.

**5** What happens to your building? Does it stay standing?

**TRY THIS!** Use other types of building material to make a new model. What can you do to make your building more secure?

18

# PROJECT!

## MODEL EARTH'S LAYERS

**SUPPLIES**

* 4 different colors of clay
* knife
* science journal

Scientists often make models of the things they study to better understand difficult concepts. This is especially useful when studying something we can't actually see, such as the inside of the earth! Make a model of the earth's layers so you can better understand what's beneath your feet.

**Caution:** Have an adult help with the knife.

1 Look at the picture on page 13. Choose one color of clay and make a small ball. This is your core.

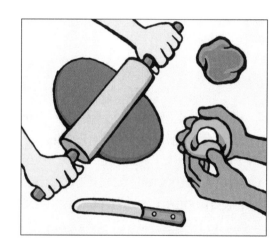

2 Choose another color of clay and flatten it. Wrap it around the clay core. What layer is this?

3 Do the same with your next two colors and name the layers of the earth you are making. On the outermost layer, sketch some landmasses.

**TRY THIS!** Use a plastic straw to drill through your model and pull out a **core sample**. This is a tube-like sample of the stuff that's buried. Scientists use core samples to study places underground that they can't travel to.

4 Have an adult use the knife to carefully slice your model in half. What do you see? Draw your model in your science journal and label the parts.

**WORDS TO KNOW**

**core sample:** a section from deep within something, such as a tree or glacier, that is taken by drilling for scientific investigation.

# PROJECT!

## EDIBLE MOLTEN ROCK

How can something as hard and solid as rock melt? That takes very high heat! Just as a wax candle can be solid, then melt into a liquid, then harden back into a solid, so can rock! Explore how this works.

**Caution:** You'll need an adult's help with this project. Be very careful with the boiling sugar syrup!

1 Apply a coating of nonstick spray to a baking sheet and set it aside.

2 Mix together the sugar, water, and corn syrup in a saucepan. With an adult's help, heat the mixture to boiling over medium-high heat. Be sure to stir it occasionally so the mixture doesn't burn or stick to the bottom of the saucepan. Once the mixture starts boiling, reduce the heat to medium and stir it frequently.

3 If you have one, use a candy thermometer to measure the temperature, heating the mixture until it's 270 degrees Fahrenheit. If you're not using a candy thermometer, test the temperature by dropping a few drops of the syrup into very cold water. Once it separates into hard threads, it's the right temperature. You don't want to heat it more than that or you'll get brittle threads that shatter easily.

4 When the mixture reaches the right temperature, add the optional food coloring and flavoring, stirring well and remove from heat.

# PROJECT!

**5** Slowly pour the hot "liquid rock" onto the baking sheet, starting at the center of the sheet and letting it spread outward.

**6** Let it cool slightly but not completely. Have an adult test the temperature. Make sure it's cool enough to handle.

**7** Wearing food gloves to protect your hands, roll up an edge of your molten rock. Before it cools completely, it will be easy to bend and push into shapes. Make ridges, trenches, and mountains! Once it cools completely, your molten rock will be "rock hard," just like real rock! You can eat it, but be careful of your teeth.

**TRY THIS!** Design and build a city out of wooden blocks on the greased baking sheet. Make another batch of molten rock and pour it through the city. What happens to the buildings? What could you do to protect them?

# PROJECT!

## SUPPLIES

* shoebox
* scissors
* long strip of paper
* paper cup
* red marker
* sand
* string

## SEISMOMETER SUCCESS

**Scientists use** seismometers **(also called seismographs) to figure out the strength of earthquakes and to discover the location of their** epicenters. **This information can be used to keep people safe. Try building your own simple seismometer!**

**1** Stand the shoebox on one end the tall way.

**2** Cut slits on the bottom of the facing sides.

**3** Thread your strip of paper through the slits so it lies flat inside the box and sticks out at least a foot on either side.

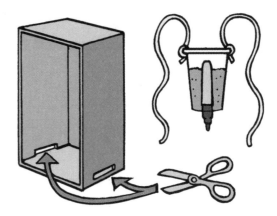

**4** Poke a hole in the bottom of the cup and slide the red marker through the hole so the tip is down. Fill the cup with enough sand so that the pen stays upright.

**5** Poke two holes in the top of the box. Poke two holes at the top of the cup on opposite sides.

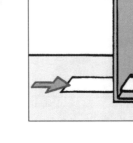

# MAKING WAVES

The energy released by an earthquake takes the form of seismic waves. These are underground waves that travel through rock, dirt, sand, and water. Body waves travel through the inside of the earth, while surface waves travel along its surface. Surface waves usually cause the most destruction.

**6** Thread the string through the holes in the cup and then thread them through the holes in the box. Adjust the string so the red marker point just touches the paper underneath. Tie the string so the cup stays where it is.

**7** You've made a seismometer! Now test it. Have a friend slam their hands on the table while you slowly slide the paper through the slits. What does the marker do? What does that show?

**TRY THIS!** Try to measure "seismic" activity on different surfaces in your house and yard. Have a friend help by stomping around! Do some surfaces transmit movement more easily than others?

## WORDS TO KNOW

**seismometer:** an instrument used to detect and record movement and vibration in the earth or other objects.

**epicenter:** the point on the earth's surface directly above the location of an earthquake.

**seismic wave:** the wave of energy that travels outward from an earthquake.

**body wave:** a seismic wave that travels through the inside of the earth.

**surface wave:** a seismic wave that travels on the surface of the earth.

# PROJECT!

## PLATE FRICTION EXPERIMENT

**In this activity you'll be able to see how tectonic plates grind against each other, building more and more tension and building up energy until they finally release that energy as an earthquake.**

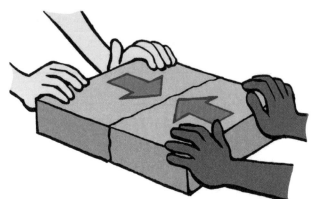

**1** Cut your foam blocks into rectangles without any round edges. Position the blocks so the long ends are lined up against each other, side by side, touching.

**2** Have a friend push one "plate" in the opposite direction you're pushing yours—either toward yours or alongside it, but in a different direction. You should both push firmly, like a backward game of tug-of-war. Consider these questions and answer them in your science journal.

* How long will the pressure keep up before one plate buckles to the other?

* What happens when the plates reach the end of their edges?

* Can you imagine how that force creates an earthquake that's felt by people—and even destroys buildings?

* How gently can you each push before the impact becomes noticeable?

**TRY THIS!** Try using blocks made from different materials. What do different blocks show you about plate movement?

## CHAPTER 2

# EVENTFUL VOLCANOES

Long ago, a giant volcano called Mount Vesuvius loomed over the cities of Herculaneum and Pompeii in the southern part of Italy. In the year 79 CE, a series of earthquakes shook the cities. The city residents didn't know it at the time, but those earthquakes were warnings about what Mount Vesuvius would soon do.

One fateful day, Mount Vesuvius exploded in a fury of volcanic lava, ash, and gases. A flow of lava known as a pyroclastic flow destroyed Herculaneum almost instantly. A few miles farther away, Pompeii was buried in volcanic ash.

**INVESTIGATE!**

How do volcanoes form?

**pyroclastic flow:** the current of lava and dirt that spreads out along the ground from a volcano after an eruption.

**vent:** an opening in the earth's crust.

**preserve:** to protect something so that it stays in its original state.

**archaeologist:** a scientist who studies ancient people and their cultures through the objects they left behind.

**WORDS TO KNOW**

Many people died the day Mount Vesuvius erupted. While powerful volcanic eruptions such as this one are rare, smaller eruptions do happen around the world. Let's take a closer look!

## HOW VOLCANOES ERUPT

Remember how the earth is made up of the core, the mantle, and the crust? A volcano forms when the liquid magma that's in the upper mantle pushes up on the crust.

Cracks called vents form in the earth's crust, and magma seeps up and out of these cracks. As millions of years pass, the volcano gets bigger and bigger as the cooled, hardened lava builds up.

## HELLO, POMPEII!

The destruction produced by the eruption of Mount Vesuvius preserved the city of Pompeii and its residents perfectly. The volcanic ash froze the city and everything in it. This allows historians and archaeologists to learn about how people lived in that time and place.

**Watch an animation of the last 48 hours of Pompeii at this website.** What do you notice?

🔎 POMPEII AEON VIDEO

Pressure forms from gases in the magma and more magma comes seeping up through the volcano. Once magma leaves the earth's crust, it is called lava and begins cooling. As lava cools and becomes solid, it forms igneous rock, adding more surface to the volcano and surrounding area.

But lava isn't the only thing to come out of volcanoes! Ash, small rocks called lapilli, and bombs, which are larger pieces of semi-molten rock that can be several feet in diameter, can also come out of volcanoes.

## TYPES OF VOLCANOES

There are four main types of volcanoes. Each type is formed a little differently and has its own unique characteristics and ways of erupting.

### CINDER CONE VOLCANOES:

Cinder cone volcanoes have one vent from which lava is spewed. The lava hardens and falls back onto the volcano as cinders. These cinders form a cone shape and a crater around the vent. Lava then flows down the face of the volcano.

PARÍCUTIN IN MEXICO, A CINDER CONE VOLCANO
CREDIT: KARLA YANNÍN ALCÁZAR QUINTERO (CC BY 2.0)

**composite volcano:** another name for a stratovolcano.

**stratovolcano:** a classic cone-shaped volcano with alternating layers of lava flows and more explosive volcanic deposits.

**caldera:** a large volcanic crater, usually formed by a large eruption that collapsed the mouth of the volcano.

## WORDS ⊚ KNOW

## COMPOSITE VOLCANOES:

Composite volcanoes, also called stratovolcanoes, are very tall and produce powerful, destructive eruptions. Mount Vesuvius is a composite volcano. The lava in this type of volcano is usually sticky. These volcanoes can have more than one vent where lava can erupt.

MOUNT ST. HELENS, A STRATOVOLCANO, ERUPTING IN 1980

## TOO HEAVY!

Yellowstone National Park is home to three calderas, which were formed between 630,000 and 2 million years ago. These look like hollowed-out craters, similar to a witch's cauldron! Calderas form when a pool of magma under a volcano empties out completely during an eruption. Sometimes, this means the ground above is too heavy to be supported and the walls of the volcano collapse, creating a caldera!

**SHIELD VOLCANOES:** Unlike stratovolcanoes, shield volcanoes erupt gently and slowly rather than with force and fury. They are named shield volcanoes because they look like a soldier's shield lying on the ground. The lava flows from shield volcanoes form a wide base composed primarily of basalt, a common igneous rock. As more rock forms, islands are born. Hawaii and Iceland are examples of islands formed through this process.

THE SIERRA GRANDE SHIELD VOLCANO IN NEW MEXICO
CREDIT: JAMES ST. JOHN (CC BY 2.0)

## UNDER THE SEA

Volcanoes can exist deep under the sea. Underwater volcanoes work slightly differently. Cracks in the sea floor allow water to flow down closer to magma. When this happens, the water becomes superheated. It's also under a huge amount of pressure! Underwater volcanoes erupt slowly and cool quickly, building up layers of igneous rock. They are also the homes of some very unusual sea creatures, such as yellow snake stars.

# NATURAL DISASTERS!

MOUNT MYOKO IN JAPAN, A LAVA DOME VOLCANO
CREDIT: OYAMA NO TAISHO

**WORDS TO KNOW**

**lava dome volcano:** a dome-shaped volcano that forms when lava breaks through the crust and mounds up.

**active volcano:** a volcano that has erupted within the past 10,000 years.

**dormant volcano:** a volcano that could still erupt, but hasn't for a long time.

**extinct volcano:** a volcano that doesn't have any magma flow anymore, so it won't erupt again.

**volcanologist:** a scientist who studies volcanoes.

**geyser:** a hot spring under pressure that shoots boiling water or steam into the air.

**LAVA DOME VOLCANOES:** Lava dome volcanoes form when very thick magma breaks through the earth's crust and piles up into a dome-like shape. The lava is too sticky and thick to spread, so it stays piled in a mound.

Volcanoes can also be active, dormant, or extinct. An active volcano has erupted within the past 10,000 years. A dormant volcano has not erupted in that timeframe, but is expected to erupt again at some point. An extinct volcano is one that volcanologists do not expect to ever erupt again.

## GEYSERS

Geysers are usually found near active volcanic areas. A geyser occurs when superheated water shoots out of gaps in the earth. It's another way the earth releases pressure.

## TYPES OF ERUPTIONS

Not all volcanoes erupt the same way. Let's take a look.

✳ **HAWAIIAN:** In this type of eruption, lava flows gently out of the vent and down the sides of the face of the volcano. This kind of eruption is common to the volcanoes of Hawaii.

✳ **STROMBOLIAN:** This type of eruption consists of tall, showy towers of lava that look a little like bright orange and red fireworks. It is named for the Stromboli Volcano in Italy, which erupts in lava shows every 20 minutes or so and has been doing this for years!

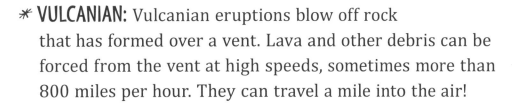

WHAT DO YOU GET WHEN YOU CROSS A VOLCANO AND A LIGHT BULB?

A lava lamp!

✳ **VULCANIAN:** Vulcanian eruptions blow off rock that has formed over a vent. Lava and other debris can be forced from the vent at high speeds, sometimes more than 800 miles per hour. They can travel a mile into the air!

✳ **PLINIAN:** This type of eruption is very powerful and loud. All of the magma fueling the volcano is released at once. Ash showers everything around the volcano for miles. This is how Mount Vesuvius in Pompeii erupted.

··· **DID YOU KNOW?** ········

A noted Roman lawyer and historian, Pliny the Younger (61–c. 113), recorded his observations about the eruption of Mount Vesuvius: "A dense dark mist seemed to be following us, spreading itself over the country like a cloud."

**ecosystem:** a community of animals and plants existing and interacting together.

**thermal imaging:** the technique of using the heat given off by an object to produce an image of it or to locate it.

**fungi:** mold, mildew, rust, and mushrooms. Plural of fungus.

**organism:** a living thing, such as an animal or a plant.

## WORDS TO KNOW

## STAYING SAFE

As you can probably tell by now, volcanoes can be huge disasters. They pose a real threat to humans and ecosystems. But people can be kept safe from volcanoes in several ways.

First, volcanologists monitor active volcanoes. These scientists gather clues to predict when a volcano might be getting ready to erupt. Volcanic eruptions often come after a series of earthquakes—even if they are small ones—so scientists use seismometers to measure earthquake activity. Plus, as a volcano gets closer to erupting, the atmosphere around the volcano can increase in temperature. Volcanologists monitor this with thermal imaging.

## BOUNCING BACK

Often, people rebuild their homes and communities around volcanoes after the danger has passed. The ecosystem surrounding the volcano must also recover. Most living things do not survive an eruption. But ecosystems do revive. Fungi are often the first organisms to return to an area. Flowers called lupines are among the first flowers able to come back because they get more of the nutrients that they need from air than soil. Animals that burrowed underground to survive, such as mice and hedgehogs, help spread seeds across the soil. The progress can be quite slow and take many decades, but an area can revive after even catastrophic eruptions.

**Take a look at Mount St. Helens as its ecosystems revive.**

— — — — — — — — →

🔍 NASA WORLD CHANGE HELENS

People who live near volcanoes must listen to volcanologists when they sound the warning that a volcano might be getting ready to erupt. They also need to listen for evacuation orders and have an evacuation plan ready so they can safely and quickly leave the area.

Sometimes, volcanoes are an important part of the tourism of an area. Hawaii is an example of this. Hiking trails give people the opportunity to see the amazing nature of volcanoes, lava flows, and volcanic rock. But tourists must also follow all volcano warnings. Often, this means sticking to hiking trails instead of going off-course. It's vital to stay away from lava flows.

**? CONSIDER AND DISCUSS**

**It's time to consider and discuss:** How do volcanoes form?

Volcanoes are a frightening example of the damage done with high heat. In the next chapter, we'll look at a much different type of natural disaster—floods!

# PROJECT!

## PLATE TECTONICS IN A PAN

Heat in the earth's interior sets the tectonic plates in motion and creates volcanic activity. That's hard to imagine, but in this activity, you're going to demonstrate how heat beneath the earth's surface breaks apart and moves the earth's crust.

**SUPPLIES**

✳ milk
✳ saucepan
✳ hot plate or stove
✳ cocoa powder
✳ timer
✳ science journal and pencil

**Caution:** Have an adult help with the stove.

**1** Pour a layer of milk to cover the bottom of the saucepan. Set the saucepan on the hot plate or stove top burner. Cover the milk with a thick layer of cocoa powder.

**2** Turn the heat to its lowest temperature. Start a timer running. Every two minutes, make notes in your science journal on what you observe.

- How much time passed before you noticed any changes taking place?

- Where did the first changes take place— around the edges or at the center?

- Why did the changes take place there first?

## ⋯ DID YOU KNOW? ⋯⋯

Where can you find the most volcanic activity in our solar system? On one of Jupiter's moons, Io! Io's surface is constantly changing because of all the volcanic activity.

**THINK ABOUT IT:** How is what you observe in the saucepan similar to what takes place in the earth's crust?

# DELICIOUS DISASTER

**Why not make a cake that's a dessert and a science experiment all in one?**

**Caution:** Have an adult help with the stove.

**1** Put the baked cake on top of the cookie sheet, round side up. Scoop out some frosting into a bowl and add brown food coloring. Do the same to make green and red frosting. Frost the cake brown for the volcano. Use green around the bottom edges for grass and red for lava around the opening.

**2** Set your cup inside the hole of the cake, so that the very top of the cup just reaches the top of the opening. If you need to, put the cup on an inverted cup, or a stack of cookies, or anything that brings it to the right height.

**3** Mix the red gelatin according to the package directions, and let it cool for about 15 minutes. You don't want it to firm up, but you don't want it steaming hot, either.

**4** Use the funnel to fill the cup halfway with the gelatin. Then, add lemon juice until it's almost full.

**5** When you're ready, drop the baking soda into the cup. Your family and friends will be amazed!

**TRY THIS!** In your science journal, sketch what happened when you dropped the baking soda into the gelatin mixture. What kind of volcanic eruption would this make? Check back in the chapter to find a description that fits!

# PROJECT!

## EDIBLE MODEL

**You can show your friends and family the different types of volcanoes with this project.**

**Caution:** Have an adult help with the microwave.

**SUPPLIES**

* microwave-safe bowl
* 4 cups miniature marshmallows or about 40 regular marshmallows
* 3 tablespoons margarine or butter
* large mixing spoon
* large mixing bowl
* 6 cups puffed rice cereal
* waxed paper
* frosting
* red food coloring

**1** In a microwave-safe bowl, melt the butter and marshmallows for two minutes. Stir, heat for another minute, and stir again.

**2** In a very large bowl, mix together the marshmallow mixture and the rice cereal until the cereal is completely coated.

**3** Put some butter on your hands to keep the cereal from sticking to your hands. Then, put a big pile of the mixture onto a large piece of waxed paper. Begin shaping the pile into one of the types of volcanoes—a cone, shield, or stratovolcano. Be sure to clearly make a crater in the top.

**4** Tint your frosting red for lava. Then "paint" it on your volcano, coming from the crater and running down the sides—just like flowing lava!

**5** Enjoy your creation and be sure to explain all about volcanoes to everyone who admires it!

**TRY THIS!** Build a village out of Lego bricks around your dessert volcano. Depending on how the lava is erupting, which way should the townspeople evacuate? What else can these imaginary people do to save themselves?

# PROJECT!

## GOOD GROWTH

**SUPPLIES**

* cardboard shoebox
* soil from three different areas, such as a beach, the woods, a playground
* seeds from a fast-growing plant, such as beans
* sticky notes
* toothpicks

One reason people settle near volcanoes—even knowing they might erupt someday—is because the soil near volcanoes is very good for growing crops. Plants grow really well in soil that has a lot of minerals because they have nutrients that plants need. Even though you might not live near a volcano, you can still test different types of soil and see how well they support life.

1 Divide your shoebox into three sections. Put the dirt samples a few inches thick in each section. Label where each section of dirt came from by writing the location on a sticky note and wrapping that sticky note around a toothpick to make a little flag. You can plant each flag in the section where it belongs.

2 Follow the instructions on the seed package to plant your seeds in all three soil samples. Water and check your seeds every day and keep track of which section sprouts first. Which seeds grow more quickly? Which soil is best for the seeds?

**TRY THIS!** Which soil sample has the most minerals? Was that sample from a spot where lots of people gathered or from a place that was mostly left alone, such as the woods?

3 Observe the seeds for a few weeks. Once they're quite tall, you can transplant them outside or into a larger pot.

**WORDS TO KNOW**

**minerals:** nutrients found in rocks and soil that keep plants and animals healthy and growing.

**nutrients:** substances in food, water, and soil that living things need to live and grow.

37

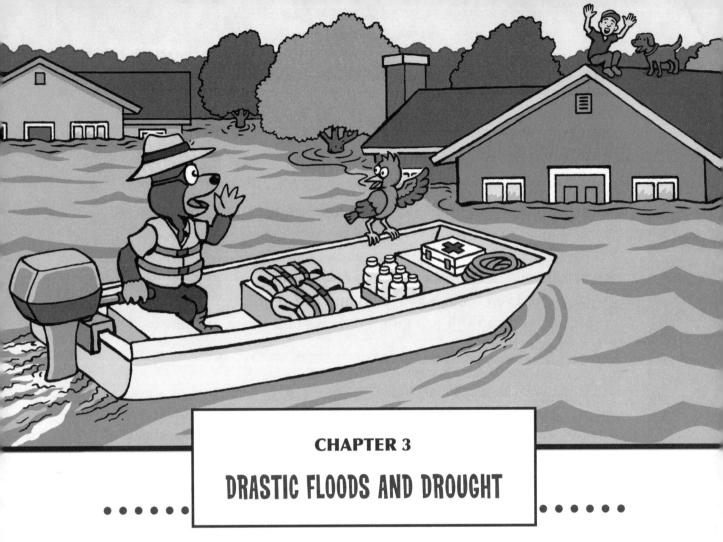

# CHAPTER 3

# DRASTIC FLOODS AND DROUGHT

**Which is better to have, too much water or too little water? That's a trick question, because both floods and droughts can be devastating natural disasters.**

When too much water is in a place at one time, rivers and streams can overflow and all that water can creep into homes and businesses, causing lots of damage. But when too little precipitation falls for a long time, the land can dry up and the living things that depend on that water can suffer.

Let's take a closer look at each type of disaster.

**? INVESTIGATE!**

Why are rivers important?

## THE WATER CYCLE

Water on Earth is always in motion and always changing from liquid to solid to gas. The water cycle describes that movement. It starts with liquid water evaporating, or turning into water vapor, which is a gas. The water vapor condenses into liquid precipitation in the form of rain, snow, hail, or sleet.

That precipitation falls to Earth and is absorbed by the ground, frozen into glaciers, or collected in ponds, lakes, streams, and rivers, where it is carried back out to the oceans. The cycle begins again.

When precipitation falls, most of the water makes its way to a river and then to the ocean. Rivers are channels for water to drain to the sea—they do a remarkable job of making sure water goes where it's supposed to! Plus, rivers give us water for drinking and irrigation. They act as a kind of "road," leading from one place to the next, offering up food to eat, and much more.

**water cycle:** the natural recycling of water through evaporation, condensation, precipitation, and collection.

**evaporate:** to change from a liquid to a gas.

**condense:** to change from a gas to a liquid.

**glacier:** a huge mass of ice and snow.

**irrigation:** the watering of land, often for crops.

**WORDS ⊙ KNOW**

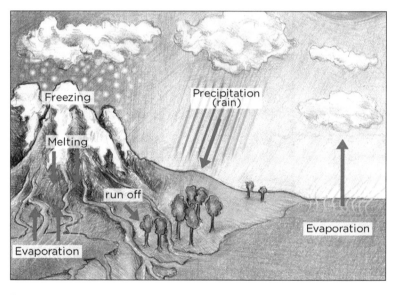

**DIAGRAM OF THE WATER CYCLE**
CREDIT: SIYAVULA EDUCATION (CC BY 2.0)

## FLOODS

Sometimes, there is too much water for a river to handle. This might happen during a storm, when far more rain than usual falls in an area during a short period of time. If the storm comes after a very dry period when very little rain has fallen, it can be especially dangerous.

Think of a kitchen sponge. When the sponge is damp, it can bend, be squished, and absorb water easily. Now, picture a sponge that is dry as a bone. What happens when you try to squeeze it? How long do you need to run it under water for it to bend easily?

The ground behaves much like a sponge. When it gets dried out, it can't handle all the rain from a storm. That means much more water than usual gets drained into the rivers. That can be overwhelming for the riverbanks, and then—flood!

**dam:** a strong barrier built across a stream or river to hold back water.

## WORDS ⊙ KNOW

Another cause of flooding is dam failure. Dams are structures that are built across rivers to hold back water for various reasons. Sometimes, dams have power plants that transform energy from running water into electricity for people to use. Other times, dams are built to create a lake. When a dam breaks and all the water that was once held back is suddenly allowed to flow naturally, any buildings in its way are in trouble.

One of the worst floods in U.S. history happened on May 31, 1889, in Johnstown, Pennsylvania. The South Fork Dam on the Little Conemaugh River, 14 miles upstream from Johnstown, burst during a heavy rainfall. The residents of Johnstown were overwhelmed with more than 3,698 gallons of water! More than 2,000 people lost their lives.

MAIN STREET IN JOHNSTOWN, PENNSYLVANIA, AFTER THE DEVASTATING FLASH FLOOD DUE TO DAM FAILURE, 1889

**crops:** plants grown as food, especially fruits, vegetables, and grains.

**flash flood:** a sudden rush of water onto an area of land that is normally dry.

**arroyo:** a steep-sided gully.

## WORDS ⊚ KNOW

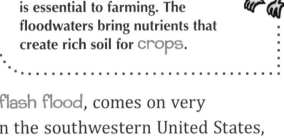

···· **DID YOU KNOW?** ·······

In some areas of the world, natural river flooding is essential to farming. The floodwaters bring nutrients that create rich soil for **crops.**

One kind of flood, called a flash flood, comes on very suddenly with no warning. In the southwestern United States, dry stream beds, called arroyos, make great places to hike. But when flash floods occur in arroyos and steep-sided, narrow canyons, they are especially dangerous.

One part of a canyon may have clear skies and sunshine, while massive amounts of rain might be pouring down a few miles upstream. All that water has no place to go but through the canyon. Hikers can be caught in the path of the sudden flood.

FLOODING IN GALENA, ALASKA, 2013
CREDIT: ALASKA DOT&PF (CC BY 2.0)

Floods are dangerous, not only because of the water. Even as the water dries up, danger still lurks in the form of mold, famine, and diseases. When an area floods, buildings that get wet are often the perfect place for mold to grow, which is very unhealthy for people to breathe.

Floods often wipe out crops, which means less food for people. And when floodwater combines with materials from sewer systems, farms, or factories, it can contaminate drinking water and make people very sick.

## DROUGHT

The flipside of too much water is too little water! Droughts are periods of time when very little precipitation falls on a region and water levels dip below normal.

What makes drought a natural disaster? Although droughts are far less dramatic than earthquakes, volcanoes, or floods, they can still be very dangerous and costly to people. When drought is very bad, people can die from it. Crops need water to grow. Animals need water to stay healthy. People need water to drink and bathe. We need water to live!

**See which regions in the United States are experiencing drought right now by looking at this interactive map.**

🔍 U.S. DROUGHT MONITOR

# NATURAL DISASTERS!

During the 1930s in the middle region of the United States, a terrible drought caused what's now known as the Dust Bowl. A lack of rain led to huge and terrible dust storms as the wind swept away the loose topsoil, which had no moisture or plantings to hold it in place. Many people and livestock died from either starvation or breathing difficulties caused by the dust.

More than 500,000 people were left homeless. Millions left the region to try and find work and a better life in the western part of the country.

## DID YOU KNOW?

Between 1876 and 1879, as many as 13 million people are believed to have died in northern China from famine after three years of drought.

A FARMING FAMILY DURING A DUST STORM, 1936
CREDIT: ARTHUR ROTHSTEIN

## STAYING SAFE

What can you do to stay safe from floods and droughts? Engineers work hard to design systems that keep rivers flowing as they should. Plus, scientists work together during heavy rainstorms to monitor water levels. As those levels get higher, warnings are sent out so people can evacuate to higher ground.

If caught in a flood, move to higher ground or higher floors. Never try to walk or swim or drive through floodwaters. Just 6 inches of water can knock you down!

If you live in an area that is experiencing drought or tends to be very dry, you can practice water conservation. To conserve water, think before you pour any down the drain.

The water you use to wash your face is just fine for feeding a plant! Didn't finish your glass of water? Save it for later. And, of course, turn off the faucet while you brush your teeth so all that water isn't going to waste.

In the next chapter, we'll get back to the hot stuff and take a look at wildfires!

WHAT DID THE FLOOD SAY?

*Nothing, it just waved!*

**CONSIDER AND DISCUSS**

**It's time to consider and discuss:** Why are rivers important?

# ABSORB!

**If the ground is dry and parched, heavy rain won't be absorbed as fast as it should be to avoid flash floods. What type of earthy material is the most absorbent? You may want to do this project outside, since it could get a little messy!**

## SUPPLIES

* small clay plant pots with drain holes (all the same size) or paper cups
* saucers for each pot or cup
* different types of earthy material such as dirt, sand, peat, clay, potting soil, gravel
* measuring cup
* water
* science journal and pencil

**1** If you're using paper cups, poke a dime-sized hole in the bottom of each one.

**2** Fill each pot or cup with a different earthy material. Don't pack it in too tight, but be sure it's nice and firm. Set the containers onto their own saucers.

**3** When you're ready, pour the same amount of water into each container. The amount of water you'll need depends on the size of your container. You want to use enough water so that it soaks well into the materials, but not so much that the soil is spilling out. Leave the containers overnight.

**4** One at a time, carefully lift each container and pour any water in the saucer into the measuring cup. In your journal, write down how much drained out of each pot. Which material absorbed the most water? Which absorbed the least?

**TRY THIS!** Repeat the experiment using rocky material instead of earthy material. What are the results? Which kind of material might be best used to create roads?

# GOOD FLOODS

**Flooding can leave behind rich soil to grow crops. With this project, simulate a flood and grow your own crops.**

## SUPPLIES

* foil
* cookie sheet
* blue aquarium rocks (optional)
* potting soil
* grass seed
* water

**1** Tear off a long, skinny piece of foil. Fold it to form a little river that is deep enough to hold some water, but no taller than the sides of your cookie sheet. Lay your river on the cookie sheet any way you want—through the middle, curvy, or diagonal. You can fill your river with blue aquarium rocks.

**2** Fill the area around the foil with potting soil. Be careful not to get the soil into your river. Pat it down firmly. Sprinkle some grass seed in the soil and cover it gently with a little more soil.

**3** Flood your land by pouring water into your river. Keep filling it until it overflows its banks and floods onto your land. When you think the flood has watered your seeds enough, stop pouring. Put the cookie sheet in the sun until the soil is dry. Then, flood your river again. Check the results in few days. What happens?

**TRY THIS!** Ancient Egyptians planted their seeds after floodwaters receded. They had to figure out a way to trap some of the floodwater to irrigate their crops later, when the soil dried up. Try changing this project to collect some of the floodwater you pour into your river. How do you do it?

# PROJECT!

## DEVASTATING DROUGHT

**See just how devastating it is when plants are denied water during a drought. But in this case, you'll still be able to use them after your project!**

**1** Lay your fresh herbs out in a single layer on the paper towels and set them all on a flat tray.

**2** Position the tray by a sunny window. Check on the herbs every few hours. How fast do they dry out? Do some dry faster than others? Record the results in your journal.

**3** When your herbs are totally dry, store them in small glass spice jars. Use them with the other spices in your kitchen when your family cooks.

**TRY THIS!** What happens if you put the herbs in the shade instead of the sun? Do they dry faster if exposed to heat (such as from the direct light of a desk lamp)? How much can they dry out and still be brought back to life a little bit with a spray of water? Some plants tolerate drought better than others.

# PROJECT!

## BUILD A DAM

**Can you design and build a dam that keeps water from flooding the area on one side of the dam?**

**SUPPLIES**

* long, shallow, clear plastic container
* sand
* popsicle sticks
* small rocks or gravel
* water

**1** Fill the plastic container about halfway with sand. Dig a path for your river through the sand.

**2** Use the popsicle sticks and small rocks to build a dam somewhere across the river.

**3** Test your dam by pouring water on one side of the dam. Did any water make it through to the other side?

**4** Make changes to your dam until you can keep most of the water on one side of the dam.

**THINK ABOUT IT:** Rivers have currents. What would happen to your dam if you added a current to your model, such as water from a hose? Would your dam be strong enough to keep the water behind it? What changes would you make to deal with the current and still keep your dam working?

**WORDS TO KNOW**

**current:** the steady flow of water in one direction.

49

# PROJECT!

## BEAT THE FLOOD

**Engineers are always trying to think of new ways to keep people and buildings safe during disasters. Put your mind to work figuring out how to solve the problem of flooding in a home!**

**SUPPLIES**

* large, flat plastic container
* modeling clay
* science journal and pencil
* building materials, such as popsicle sticks, blocks, recycled plastic containers, cardboard, sponges, cloth
* jug of water

**1** Imagine that you are designing a house that will be built near the banks of a river. In your container, create the house site by heaping the modeling clay at one end and gradually sloping it toward the other end. Make sure the modeling clay doesn't go more than a third of the way up the side of the box.

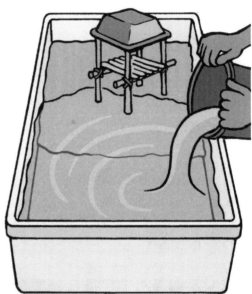

**2** In your science journal, draw some ideas about how you can build a house that will be safe even if the river rises. How will you make sure the people who live there can evacuate? Can you design a house that can withstand flooding? How will you make the house livable in both wet and dry conditions?

**3** Build your model house out of your supplies. Put it on top of the modeling clay, or hillside, in your container or by the river.

# PROJECT!

## FLOATING HOMES

Engineers and architects are working hard to figure out new ways of designing buildings to survive during natural disasters. One idea is a home that floats when the waters rise! This kind of structure would be good in an area that experiences flooding without a lot of violent waves.

**You can read an article and see a video about one kind of floating home design at this website.** What other ways can you think of to keep property safe during a flood?

🔍 GREENMATTERS HOUSE FLOAT →

SOMETIMES, ENTIRE VILLAGES ARE BUILT ON STILTS TO KEEP THE HOUSES DRY!

**4** Test your design! Pour water into your plastic container so that it gradually rises over the hillside. What happens to your house? Does it stay dry? Is it watertight?

**TRY THIS!** Redesign! Every engineer goes through many different designs, so don't worry if your house doesn't hold up. Go back to your plans and use what you learned from your first try.

## CHAPTER 4

# WILDFIRE WOES

Anyone who has ever roasted marshmallows around a campfire knows that when it's safely contained, an outdoor fire can be a beautiful thing. But when fires burn out of control, they can create a massive amount of damage.

Wildfires are sometimes caused by humans and sometimes caused by nature, such as lightning. No matter the cause, destructive fires burn thousands of acres of natural habitat every year, create millions of dollars in damage to homes and property, and can even cost people their lives.

**? INVESTIGATE!**

What are some ways that wildfires can start?

Let's learn more about what causes wildfires and what we can do to prepare for and prevent them.

## HOW DO WILDFIRES HAPPEN?

There are two kinds of wildfires—either they occur naturally or they're started by people. The fires that happen naturally are usually caused by a lightning strike.

**··· DID YOU KNOW? ···**

In some places, farmers burn their fields on purpose to help crops grow.

Most wildfires happen from human mistakes. Campers do not put out a campfire properly, a hiker drops a match, or someone throws a lit cigarette on the ground.

THE 2018 CAMP FIRE IN CALIFORNIA
CREDIT: NASA (JOSHUA STEVENS)

# NATURAL DISASTERS!

**fuel:** a material used to produce heat or power by burning.

**fire triangle:** the three things needed to produce a fire—heat, oxygen, and fuel.

**ignite:** to burst into flames.

## WORDS TO KNOW

Wildfires need three things: heat, oxygen, and fuel. These are known as the "fire triangle." Heat comes from a source, such as a match or lightning. Oxygen from the air encourages flames to burn. Fuel is the dry grasses, leaves, and branches on the ground that help ignite trees and structures. Once a fire is going, it will spread in the direction where the most of these three things are available.

HOW QUICKLY CAN A WILDFIRE START?

*Lightning fast.*

## REAL-LIFE DISASTER

In November 2018, the whole world was watching California as terrible wildfires raged across the state. The Camp Fire in northern California burned more than 240 square miles, causing more than $16 billion in damage. That fire burned down the entire town of Paradise, California, and was the most destructive fire in California history. It was also the deadliest fire in 100 years in America, causing more than 80 deaths. The fire burned for 17 days before firefighters were able to completely contain it. At the same time, the Woolsey Fire was burning through southern California. That fire burned nearly 100,000 acres in 14 days. Almost 300,000 people were evacuated. The city of Malibu was severely damaged and many celebrities, including Miley Cyrus, lost their homes. Because Malibu has many farms, a lot of animals were left behind. Horses, llamas, alpacas, and more found their way through the clouds of smoke to the beaches of Malibu to try to escape the fire. The fire caused $6 billion in damage.

**Check out the National Interagency Fire Center website to see where wildfires are happening.** This government organization also uses weather patterns to predict where wildfires might start.

🔍 NATIONAL FIRE CENTER →

**ground fire:** a wildfire that burns buried vegetation.

**surface fire:** a wildfire that occurs on the surface of the ground, burning low-lying vegetation.

**crown fire:** a forest fire that moves at great speed across treetops.

**climate:** the average weather in an area during a long period of time.

**Santa Ana winds:** strong, dry winds that start inland and blow toward the coast.

**climate change:** changes in the earth's climate patterns, including rising temperatures, which is called global warming.

**WORDS TO KNOW**

Some wildfires are ground fires—they burn buried vegetation. Surface fires have flames a few feet high. Crown fires, which burn at the tops of trees, are the most dangerous because they spread the fastest.

## WILDFIRES AROUND THE WORLD

Any area where the climate is dry and hot for long periods of time, but also wet enough to allow trees to grow, is at risk for wildfires. Forested areas in the United States and Canada often have fires. In California, strong winds called the Santa Ana winds, which blow in the fall and winter, help spread fires far and wide.

One of the main reasons that wildfires are increasing is climate change. As the global temperature rises, hot and dry climates become hotter and dryer. There is less water to put out the fires, less moisture in the air to keep the fires from spreading, stronger winds to spread the fires, and more dry tinder for fuel.

**DID YOU KNOW?**

Lightning strikes the earth more than 100,000 times each day! Between 10 and 20 percent of those strikes can cause a fire.

**brush:** low-growing plants.

**retardant:** a material that slows or stops the spread of fire.

**extinguish:** to put out a fire.

**WORDS TO KNOW**

## DID YOU KNOW?

Scientists claim that the 2018 California wildfire season was extra severe because there were so many dead trees. The Camp Fire and the Woolsey Fire had a record number of dead trees to use as fuel—more than 129 million trees drying in the sun that easily caught on fire.

When wildfires happen, specially trained teams of firefighters and forest rangers get to work. They put out the flames and use bulldozers and backhoes to clear away brush to stop the fires from spreading. Airplanes filled with water or a chemical retardant fly low over the flames to extinguish them.

A FIREFIGHTER WORKS TO BATTLE FLAMES IN A 2017 WILDFIRE IN SOUTH DAKOTA.
CREDIT: A1C DONALD C. KNECHTEL

**canopy:** an umbrella of treetops over the forest.

**WORDS** ⊙ **KNOW**

## AFTER THE FIRES

Sometimes, fire is healthy for the environment. Some ecosystems depend on fire to thin out the tree canopy. When leaves and branches become too thick, they block out sunlight and don't allow plants on the ground to grow. After a fire, the old, burned trees provide homes for birds and animals. Many new plants thrive, because weeds have been cleared away. Wildflowers, especially, bloom during this time.

Watch this video to learn more about wildfires and how we fight them.

🔎 EARTHFIX MEDIA FIGHTING WILDFIRES

# THE BEAR NECESSITIES

Have you met Smokey Bear? Smokey Bear was a real bear cub who was rescued from a New Mexico forest fire in 1950. Now, he's an American cartoon character who has taught generations of kids that "only you can prevent forest fires." It's true! The more careful humans are when they interact with nature, the fewer accidental fires there will be.

## WORDS TO KNOW

**dormant:** in a state of rest or inactivity.

**controlled burn:** a fire set to burn off extra flammable material, also called a prescribed burn.

**fire line:** a line cleared in the ground free of flammable material that a fire can't cross.

**flammable:** something that can easily burn.

### DID YOU KNOW?

In 1871, the Peshtigo fire burned more than a million acres of Wisconsin and Michigan. Thousands of lives were lost. The Peshtigo fire is considered the deadliest wildfire in U.S. history.

In fact, some plants need fire to grow! Pitch pines, which grow in the Pine Barrens of the Northeast United States, have pine cones that need fire to open up. The Jack Pines of the Great Lakes region need minerals from the soil that burned material leaves behind. Chamise, a flowering plant that grows in the western United States, grows dormant seeds that need fire to sprout.

## WHEN FIRES ARE ACTUALLY GOOD

Firefighters and forest rangers sometimes set fires on purpose. This kind of fire is called a controlled burn. When experts decide there's too much fuel on the ground in the form of dead plants and branches, they set a small, controlled fire to clear away the fuel that could start much worse fires later. Before starting a controlled burn, firefighters and forest rangers dig a fire line in the ground, clearing away any flammable materials from this line. If the fire has nothing to burn, it can't spread any farther. This way, the controlled burn stays in one area and helps lower the risk of future wildfires.

**Watch this video about a controlled burn in Iowa.** What do the firefighters do to make sure the fire is safe?

🔍 CONTROLLED BURN VIDEO IOWA

**fire-resistant:** something that doesn't burn.

**WORDS TO KNOW**

Nature bounces back quickly after a large fire—but it's not so easy for humans. Homes that have burned to the ground don't just grow back next season! In America, the Federal Emergency Management Association (FEMA) is a government agency that helps people rebuild their homes and their lives after natural disasters. Those new homes can be built to be fire-resistant to help people avoid losing their homes again.

## HOW TO BE PREPARED AND STAY SAFE

Wildfires are scary, but not every state in America is likely to have one. In general, the five states where it is most common to see wildfires are California, Georgia, Texas, North Carolina, and Florida. The five states where it is least common are Nebraska, Rhode Island, Illinois, Delaware, and Hawaii.

## YELLOWSTONE'S SUMMER OF FIRE

The summer of 1988 was unlike any other summer in Yellowstone National Park. The famous park, which spans 3,500 square miles across Wyoming, Montana, and Idaho, is home to spectacular natural wonders such as Old Faithful, the geyser that erupts every day. During that summer, wildfires raged through the park, burning almost 794,000 acres of the beautiful park before the fire was extinguished.

A BISON CROSSES A ROAD DURING THE 1988 YELLOWSTONE FIRE.

If you live in an area at great risk for wildfires, the best thing to do is keep an eye on the news. The sooner you know when danger is on its way, the safer you'll be.

Communities in states such as California have emergency notification systems to warn people when a fire is close enough to their homes that they might have to evacuate. Have an evacuation plan for the family. Talk to your family about what you would do in case of a wildfire emergency. A fire emergency kit is also a smart way to prepare.

In the next chapter, we'll look at fire's opposite, rain, as we study hurricanes!

 **CONSIDER AND DISCUSS**

**It's time to consider and discuss:** What are some ways that wildfires can start?

# PROJECT!

## FIND OUT WHERE THE FIRES ARE

**Maps are very important tools for fighting wildfires.**

**1** Go to the USDA's fire-mapping site. Where — — → in the United States are fires burning right now?

🔍 USDA FIRE MAP

**2** Write down the locations in your science journal and pick one to research. Some of the questions you might want to consider include the following.

* Why do you think a fire is burning in that one spot right now?

* What is it about the climate of that place that led to the spread of a wildfire?

* How did the geography of the place play a role?

* What can the community do to help prevent future fires there?

···· **DID YOU KNOW?** ····

**Forest fires move faster uphill than downhill! The steeper the slope, the faster the fire travels.**

**TRY THIS!** Look at fires on a world map at this NASA site. Can you see how there are more wildfires in certain parts of the world? Do some research on the climates of those areas. What do you discover?

🔍 NASA WORLDVIEW FIRE

**WORDS ᴛᴏ KNOW**

**geography:** the features of a place, such as mountains and rivers.

# PROJECT!

## ONLY YOU!

**Smokey Bear has a famous catchphrase: "Only YOU can prevent fire!" Come up with new ways of helping people to remember fire safety when hiking or camping in the woods.**

**1** With a group of friends or classmates, brainstorm some catchphrases. These can be funny, serious, even scary! Remember the following tips.

- Keep your catchphrases short so they're easy to remember.

- Try using alliteration by making most of your words start with the same sound.

- Try using rhyming to make your catchphrase fun to say out loud.

- Use familiar language.

**2** Have the group vote for their favorite catchphrase.

**3** Make posters, booklets, and even videos or podcasts using that catchphrase to educate people about fire safety.

**4** Get feedback from teachers and other adults to improve your fire safety campaign. Then, share it with other people to grow awareness about the dangers of wildfires.

**TRY THIS!** Conduct a pretend interview with Smokey Bear about his lifelong work to prevent fires.

**WORDS to KNOW**

**alliteration:** the repetition of a sound at the beginning of two or more neighboring words, such as "zany zebras" or "babbling brook."

# INTERVIEW A FIREFIGHTER

**Firefighters work hard to keep people and communities safe, not just when there's a wildfire, but all year round. To really understand the job, visit a firehouse and interview a firefighter!**

**1** Ask an adult to help you contact a firefighter and to stay with you as you conduct an interview.

**2** Contact your local firehouse and politely ask to make an appointment to visit. Be sure to mention you'd like to ask a firefighter some questions about their work.

**3** Prepare a list of five or so questions. Some ideas include the following.

- What is it like to battle a wildfire? Is it different from fighting a house fire?

- What do you like best about your job?

- Why did you choose this job?

- What's the most challenging part about being a firefighter?

**4** On the day of your visit, show up at the scheduled time. You might get a tour of the firehouse and the firetrucks! Ask your questions. If allowed, you can even take pictures. Take notes on the firefighter's responses. If you want to record their answers with a recording device, ask permission first.

**5** After your visit, send a thank you letter!

**TRY THIS!** Record the interview on a phone or digital recorder and create a radio show about your visit to the firehouse!

# PROJECT!

## FIRE LINE TEST

**SUPPLIES**

* tissue paper or newspaper
* large, shallow pan
* spray bottle
* water
* red food coloring
* science journal and pencil

**One of the ways that firefighters battle wildfires is by digging a fire line. Here's how you can create a test fire line.**

**1** Shred the tissue paper or newspaper into small pieces and scatter them in the pan. Distribute them evenly across the pan until the layer is about an inch thick.

**2** Run your finger through the shredded paper to dig out a trench. You want to create an area without any shredded paper.

**3** Fill your spray bottle with water and add a few drops of red food coloring—this will be your fire. Squirt one side of your fire line. This represents the fire burning. You don't need to squirt much—the water will spread through the tissue paper or newspaper by itself, just like a growing fire.

## HERE, KITTY, KITTY, KITTY

Have you ever seen a cute picture of a firefighter rescuing a cat that's stuck in a tree? Thanks to picture books, this is an image many people have of what firefighters do at their job. And, in some places, you might be able to find a firefighter to help get a cat out of a tree, More often, they'll say no to bringing their ladder truck while on duty. For one thing, ladder trucks are pretty complicated vehicles that are usually used for reaching far higher than a cat in a tree. Plus, what happens if an emergency call comes in while the truck and team are trying to rescue a cat?

**4** What happens when it reaches your fire line? Just like a fire, the water stops spreading. If it doesn't work, ask yourself why, and see what you can do to change the results.

### DID YOU KNOW?

Wild animals are very good at staying safe during wildfires. They run or fly away or burrow underground to escape the flames!

**TRY THIS!** Spray water more heavily on the center shredded paper and see what happens when your "fire" rages even more. Record your observations in your science journal.

## PROJECT!

# ESCAPE!

### SUPPLIES

- * paper
- * marker
- * computer (optional)
- * copier or printer

**If you live in an area with the potential for wildfires, you want to be sure to have a fire escape plan in place with your family. But even if your home isn't likely to be threatened by wildfire, having a home fire escape plan is a great idea. It can keep your family safe in case of a house fire, too.**

**1** On the paper, in an upper corner, write the number for your local fire department with the marker. Then, draw a diagram of the floor plan of your house. If you'd rather create this on the computer, you can do that instead. Be sure to draw in all doors and windows.

**2** Mark the location of all the smoke alarms in the house. You should have one in each bedroom, one in the hall outside the bedrooms, and one on every level of the house. Don't forget the basement if you have one!

## COLD HEAT

You might not think of wildfires raging in the Arctic, where it's very cold for much of the year, but they do! However, because of climate change, these fires are changing their patterns. They are far more frequent, bigger, and hotter. In recent years, wildfires in the far north have caused much more damage than in the past. This can change entire ecosystems, affecting every creature that lives there and the quality of the air for many miles.

# PROJECT!

**3** Call a family meeting. Explain the importance of having a fire safety plan for the family in case of an emergency.

**4** Work together, using your diagram, to identify TWO ways out of each room. If you find that an upstairs window is one option, be sure to have a fire safety ladder in that room or have a plan to get down from there.

**5** Pick a safe family place outside to meet. You might want to meet on a neighbor's porch (ask them first, of course!) or by a big tree that's away from the house.

**6** Practice your evacuation plan at least twice a year.

**TRY THIS!** When a wildfire threatens, whole towns might have to be evacuated! Get a map of your town and figure out which roads to take to be safe. Ask an adult to help. There might be an official evacuation path you need to follow. Remember, though, this route might change depending on where the fire is, so always listen for official updates on the news.

# CHAPTER 5

# HURRICANES AND TORNADOES

**Have you ever experienced a hurricane or tornado? These storms are both very windy, though they happen over very different parts of the land.**

Hurricanes have lots of rainfall and winds that can blow up to 200 miles per hour. They often last for many hours, even days, and can cause major destruction, flooding, and death.

But hurricanes are actually important for the health and well-being of the earth. Let's see why.

**? INVESTIGATE!**

Why are hurricanes important to the health of the planet?

First, let's talk terms. People use many different terms for hurricanes and for the storms that develop into hurricanes. You might hear a storm referred to as a hurricane, a typhoon, or a cyclone. These are all the same thing!

**DID YOU KNOW?**

The places in the United States that are most likely to be hit with hurricanes are the Atlantic coast and Hawaii. Florida gets the most hurricanes of any state—more than 120 hurricanes have hit the Sunshine State!

The only difference is where in the world the storm occurs. In general, the storms in the Atlantic Ocean are called hurricanes, storms in the Pacific Ocean are called typhoons, and storms in the Indian Ocean are called tropical cyclones.

HURRICANE OLAF, 2015
CREDIT: NASA IMAGE BY JEFF SCHMALTZ, LANCE/EOSDIS RAPID RESPONSE

**eye:** the calm and peaceful center of a hurricane.

**atmosphere:** the blanket of air surrounding the earth.

**tropical storm:** a very strong storm that forms in the tropics.

## WORDS ⊙ KNOW

## THE CYCLE OF A HURRICANE

A hurricane forms over tropical ocean water. Warmth and water are the two main ingredients of a hurricane. Warm, moist air rises up, and cooler air moves in to replace it. The cooler air then begins to warm and rise. This cycle causes big storm clouds to form and move in a spiral pattern.

The storm starts to spin faster and faster and an eye forms in the center. Inside the eye, it is very calm, but just around the eye, the storm is the most severe. This is where warm air rushes up from the ocean and where cold air sinks down from the atmosphere, keeping the spiral movement going. The storm is now called a tropical storm.

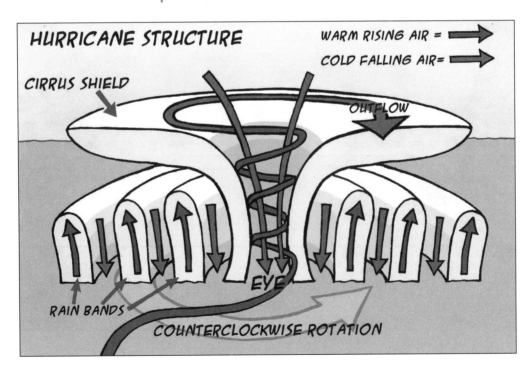

HURRICANE STRUCTURE

WARM RISING AIR =

COLD FALLING AIR=

CIRRUS SHIELD

OUTFLOW

EYE

RAIN BANDS

COUNTERCLOCKWISE ROTATION

**meteorologist:** a person who studies the science of weather and climate.

**WORDS ⊙ KNOW**

Once the winds from the tropical storm reach 74 miles per hour, it is officially a hurricane. The whole storm—clouds, moisture, and wind—moves over the ocean until it either reaches cooler waters and breaks apart or touches down on land.

(PS) **Watch this National Geographic video to learn more about hurricanes.**

— — — — — — — →

🔎 YOUTUBE HURRICANES 101 2018

A hurricane doesn't stay together long once it hits land. It loses its supply of warm air and water vapor and begins to lose strength. Its winds slow, the rain stops falling, and the storm finally ends.

Sometimes, hurricanes lose wind speed but still dump lots of water on the ground below. This happens when a hurricane stalls near a source of water vapor—that water vapor is fuel for the storm.

## HOW STORMS ARE NAMED

Hurricanes are the only natural disasters that get a name. So many hurricanes form every hurricane season that meteorologists need a quick and simple way to keep track of them. The World Meteorological Organization has the job of naming hurricanes. It has a list of male and female names that are used every six years. At the beginning of each hurricane season, meteorologists start with a name at the beginning of the alphabet. The names of especially damaging hurricanes, however, are never used again out of respect for the people who lost their lives.

These storms can cause extreme flooding. On the coast, which is where hurricanes tend to hit hardest, the rough ocean waters send powerful waves crashing onto the shore. Houses and cars—and even entire hotels—have been destroyed this way.

## DID YOU KNOW?

In the Northern Hemisphere—the part of the world north of the equator—the winds of a cyclone rotate counterclockwise. In the Southern Hemisphere—south of the equator—the winds move clockwise.

This is what happened when Hurricane Harvey hit eastern Texas in 2017. Harvey stalled over the coastline of eastern Texas and the warm waters of the Gulf of Mexico. In an average September, that region of Texas receives 3 to 4 inches of rain. During just four days, 40 to 60 inches of rain fell!

HURRICANE ISABEL IN 2003

# HOW STRONG WAS HURRICANE KATRINA?

The strength of a hurricane is measured by what's called the Saffir-Simpson Hurricane Scale. You might hear meteorologists refer to a Category 1, 2, 3, 4, or 5 hurricane—but what does that mean? It has to do with wind speed and how much damage a storm can cause. Categories 1 and 2 are dangerous storms with high winds that can cause damage to homes. Category 3 storms and above are considered "major" storms with winds of more than 110 miles per hour, which result in major damage and can result in loss of life.

When Hurricane Katrina hit New Orleans, Louisiana, in 2005, it was the strongest storm to make landfall in America in more than 35 years. The Category 5 hurricane claimed more than 1,800 lives and resulted in the most expensive disaster recovery in the country. The storm originated in the Bahamas, made landfall in Florida as a Category 1 hurricane, crossed the state, and hit the Gulf of Mexico. Once it landed on the water again, the hurricane quickly gained strength and became a Category 5.

By the time the storm was over, 80 percent of New Orleans was underwater. New Orleans is below sea level, which means that it tends to collect water rather than drain water. Emergency crews worked to rescue people by helicopter and by boat, helped by volunteers who did whatever they could. It took 46 days to pump  all the water out of the city. By that time, many neighborhoods were covered in mold from water and hot temperatures and had to be rebuilt from the ground up. New Orleans is still recovering from this devastating storm.

## MOVING HEAT

What do hurricanes, cyclones, and typhoons have to do with keeping the planet livable? These violent storms have the very important job of moving heat from one area to another! They suck up a whole lot of warmth over the tropical oceans and move that warmth northward to colder regions.

Without these storms, hot regions would be too hot and cold regions would be too cold. People and other living things wouldn't be able to live in those areas. While hurricanes are dangerous and cause a lot of damage, our planet would be a much different place without them.

## TORNADO!

Have you ever seen *The Wizard of Oz*? Remember the tornado and how it destroys much of Dorothy's home in Kansas?

Tornadoes are very real natural disasters, and most of them happen in the Great Plains of the North American continent. They form from thunderstorms. Luckily, fewer than 10 percent of thunderstorms create tornadoes.

Scientists don't know exactly why tornadoes form, but they do know tornadoes are made up of two columns of air that begin in a thunderstorm. In one column, warm, moist air rises until it reaches high enough that the air begins to cool. The water vapor condenses, forming clouds that spread out across the sky. The water vapor turns into cold water droplets, which create rain or hail that falls to the ground. This is the second column.

These columns feed off each other and spin faster, becoming more powerful. Eventually, they might turn into the spinning disaster known as a tornado. Just as in a hurricane, there is a calm space in the center of the spinning air of a tornado called the eye of the storm.

Most tornadoes last less than 10 minutes! You might think they can't do a lot of damage in such a short time, but that's not true. When tornadoes touch down on the ground, they act like gigantic vacuum cleaners. The rotating air sucks things up into the core and then throws them back out.

**DID YOU KNOW?**

In 2018, there were at least 1,123 tornadoes formed in the United States. Some tornadoes were also spotted in Italy, France, Brazil, Germany, Canada, Japan, and Australia.

Houses can be ripped off the ground and tossed around like blocks. Trees, telephone poles, cars, boulders—the tornado is stronger than all.

Many people think of tornadoes as being a funnel shape, but they actually come in many different shapes. A tornado can be a wedge shape with straight sides, wider than it is tall, or it might be very long and skinny. Most tornadoes are gray, but sometimes they look white.

## STAYING SAFE DURING TORNADOES AND HURRICANES

The most important thing you can do if your town sends a warning that a tornado might form is seek shelter. Many homes in states where tornadoes happen have underground storm shelters. You can also find shelter in a basement. Head for a closet or bathroom if you don't have a basement.

With hurricanes, you have more warning. Hurricanes usually form during a certain season. In the United States, hurricane season is June through November.

## BAD STORM

During one day and night in 2011, 216 tornadoes touched down in Mississippi and Alabama. In one town, a tornado peeled the pavement right off the roads and made a deep trench in the ground. In another town, tornadoes turned solid brick homes into piles of rubble. Tornadoes stripped the bark off of trees, injured 1,500 people, and killed 65 more. The storm that gave rise to these tornadoes lasted three days and caused the most expensive tornado damage in history.

WHAT DID THE TORNADO SAY TO THE TOWN?

I have my eye on you!

Just as with other natural disasters, be prepared by having an evacuation bag already packed in case you need to leave your house quickly. Many people tape or board the windows of buildings so the strong winds are less likely to smash them. It's also a good idea to put valuable things in places where they're less likely to get broken.

Since flooding often follows hurricanes, have a plan for watching the water level and evacuating before it gets too high. Remember, never walk or drive through water, even if you think it's only a few inches deep. It can get much deeper very quickly, and even just a few inches of water can flow fast enough to sweep people and things away.

### DID YOU KNOW?

During an average hurricane season in the Atlantic Ocean, about 12 tropical storms that can turn into hurricanes form.

Now, you know a lot about the different natural disasters that can hit people and communities around the world. The most important thing to be aware of whenever you are facing a storm, eruption, wildfire, or some other natural disaster, is to be safe. Prepare for danger by packing an evacuation kit, having a family plan, and listening to people in charge.

Natural disasters are extremely rare, but it's always good to know what to do in the event one happens in your neighborhood!

### ? CONSIDER AND DISCUSS

**It's time to consider and discuss:** Why are hurricanes important to the health of the planet?

# PROJECT!

## FEEL THE WIND

**Wind is a big part of a hurricane! In fact, without wind, there is no hurricane. Meteorologists use high-tech anemometers to measure wind speed. In its simplest form, however, an anemometer is nothing more than cups that rotate on a center shaft and catch the wind. Each full rotation that the cups make is the equivalent of one mile per hour of wind speed. Make one yourself!**

**1** Take four paper cups and punch a single hole halfway down the side of each cup. Paint one cup a different color from the others.

**2** On the fifth cup, make four holes evenly spaced around the rim. The first and third holes should be slightly closer to the rim than the second and fourth holes. Carefully punch one hole in the center of the bottom of this cup.

**3** Slide two of the dowels through the holes in the fifth cup to make an X. Make sure the first four cups are all on their sides facing the same direction. Connect each through the hole in its side to an end of each of the dowels. Secure each cup to its dowel with tape. Why do they all need to face the same direction?

## WORDS TO KNOW

**anemometer:** a weather instrument that measures wind speed.

**shaft:** a short rod that allows something to spin.

# PROJECT!

**4** Insert a dowel through the hole in the bottom of the fifth cup until it meets the X. Tape the X and the center dowel together.

**5** Place the center dowel in the empty water bottle and let the center cup rest on top. Blow into one of the cups to test if your anemometer is working. Then, take your anemometer outside to see if it works in the wind. Why did we make one cup different from the others?

**6** In your journal, record how many rotations your anemometer makes in 30 seconds. What changes can you make to it to make it spin faster? Record your ideas in your science journal.

**TRY THIS!** Design a different anemometer. Does it work better than the original anemometer? Why? How do you know if it works better?

# PROJECT!

## HURRICANE MODEL

**SUPPLIES**

* paper clip
* string
* large, round bowl of water
* spoon

**With this project, you can see how wind movement varies depending on where it is within a hurricane.**

**1** Tie the paper clip to the string.

**2** Stir the water around in the bowl in one direction until you have a steady whirlpool going. This simulates the hurricane's winds swirling around.

**3** Holding the end of the string, drop the paper clip into the water near the edge of the bowl. Does it get caught up in the moving water? This is what happens to anything that is in the winds in the outer band of a hurricane.

**4** Pull out the paper clip. Stir the water again and lower the paper clip as close as you can to the center of the bowl. What happens? Is the paper clip moving faster or slower than when it was closer to the edge of the swirling motion?

**TRY THIS!** What does this activity show you about how winds travel in a hurricane? Where would you rather get caught in a hurricane, in the eye or toward the edge?

# WIND TUNNEL TESTS

**Test different structures and strengths of buildings with this simple wind tunnel! A wind tunnel is a place where high winds are produced on purpose.**

## SUPPLIES

* cardboard box
* scissors
* materials such as Lego blocks and popsicle sticks to make some buildings
* clay
* fan

**1** Cut out the short ends of the box, so it's solid on four sides and open on the short ends, like a tunnel.

**2** Using the building materials, make different structures that are small enough to fit inside your wind tunnel. Secure them with clay or think of other ways to hold them down. You could try taping them or propping them up with toothpicks or popsicle sticks.

**3** When you're ready, aim your fan on low speed into your wind tunnel. If your fan doesn't have speeds, start with it farther away, then move it closer to make the wind stronger. What happens to the models inside the box?

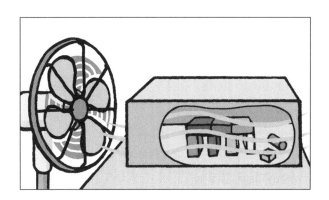

**TRY THIS!** Try different types of structures and supports with different intensities of wind. You'll see how hard it can be for real-life engineers to construct buildings that stand up to hurricane-force winds!

# MODEL A STORM SURGE

## SUPPLIES

* square plastic container with 2-inch sides
* modeling clay
* materials such as Lego blocks to make buildings
* water
* fan

A storm surge is a sudden rise of water near the coast. Storm surges are usually caused by a hurricane or other major storm. The winds of the hurricane push the water onto land, producing flooding and often destroying homes. The water can sometimes travel many miles inland! Let's see how this works. You may want to do this project outside or in a sink to avoid splashing water all over the place.

1 Shape the clay into a shoreline along one inside edge of the container. Make part of the shoreline about 1-inch high and the rest about 2 inches high.

2 Create some buildings all along your shoreline.

3 Fill the container with water so the shore is just below the buildings on the lowest part of your shoreline.

4 Aim your fan on low speed so it blows over the water toward the shoreline. If your fan doesn't have speeds, place it farther away. What happens? Turn the fan up or move it closer. What happens now? Does having some buildings higher up help to keep them safe and dry?

**TRY THIS!** What could you do to protect buildings on the shore from storm surges?

# PROJECT!

# NATURAL DISASTER CROSSWORD PUZZLE

Do this fun crossword puzzle using vocabulary from this book! Look in the glossary if you need help.

**Down**

1. A fire that spreads quickly, usually across a large area of land.

2. A prolonged period without rain, leading to dry conditions and a scarcity of fresh water.

3. A substance in food and soil that living things need to live and grow.

5. A swirling vortex of wind in a funnel shape that extends toward the earth from a large storm system.

6. A powerful storm with winds of at least 74 miles per hour.

8. The natural area where a plant or animal lives.

9. A mountain formed by magma or ash forcing its way from deep inside the earth to the surface.

**Across**

4. Rising water levels caused by factors such as rain, collapsed dams, and rising sea levels.

7. The sudden movement of pieces of the outer layer of the earth.

10. The removal of people from danger.

active volcano: a volcano that has erupted within the past 10,000 years.

adapt: to change in order to survive.

aftershock: an earthquake that happens after the initial shock.

alliteration: the repetition of a sound at the beginning of two or more neighboring words, such as "zany zebras" or "babbling brook."

anemometer: a weather instrument that measures wind speed.

archaeologist: a scientist who studies ancient people and their cultures through the objects they left behind.

arroyo: a steep-sided gully.

ash: the powder that remains after something is burned.

atmosphere: the blanket of air surrounding the earth.

basalt: a black, shiny volcanic rock.

body wave: a seismic wave that travels through the inside of the earth.

bomb: a rounded mass of lava exploded from a volcano.

boundary: the place where two plates meet.

brush: low-growing plants.

caldera: a large volcanic crater, usually formed by a large eruption that collapsed the mouth of the volcano.

canopy: an umbrella of treetops over the forest.

cinder cone volcano: a small, steep-sided volcano built by ash and small cinders.

climate: the average weather in an area during a long period of time.

climate change: changes in the earth's climate patterns, including rising temperatures, which is called global warming.

composite volcano: another name for a stratovolcano.

condense: to change from a gas to a liquid.

conservation: managing and protecting something, such as natural resources or an archaeological site.

contaminate: to pollute or make dirty.

controlled burn: a fire set to burn off extra flammable material, also called a prescribed burn.

core: the innermost layer of the earth.

core sample: a section from deep within something, such as a tree or glacier, that is taken by drilling for scientific investigation.

crops: plants grown as food, especially fruits, vegetables, and grains.

crown fire: a forest fire that moves at great speed across treetops.

crust: the earth's outermost layer.

current: the steady flow of water in one direction.

dam: a strong barrier built across a stream or river to hold back water.

disease: sickness.

dormant: in a state of rest or inactivity.

dormant volcano: a volcano that could still erupt, but hasn't for a long time.

drought: a long period without rain, leading to dry conditions and a scarcity of fresh water.

Dust Bowl: the region of the south central United States that was damaged in the 1920s and 1930s by persistent dust storms that killed off crops and livestock.

earthquake: the sudden movement of pieces of the outer layer of the earth.

ecosystem: a community of animals and plants existing and interacting together.

engineer: a person who uses science, math, and creativity to design and build things.

epicenter: the point on the earth's surface directly above the location of an earthquake.

eruption: a violent explosion of gas, steam, magma, or ash.

evacuation: the removal of people from danger.

evaporate: to change from a liquid to a gas.

extinct volcano: a volcano that doesn't have any magma flow anymore, so it won't erupt again.

extinguish: to put out a fire.

eye: the calm and peaceful center of a hurricane.

famine: a serious lack of food, resulting in starvation.

fault: a crack in the earth's crust where tectonic plates move against each other.

fire line: a line cleared in the ground free of flammable material that a fire can't cross.

fire-resistant: something that doesn't burn.

fire triangle: the three things needed to produce a fire—heat, oxygen, and fuel.

flammable: something that can easily burn.

flash flood: a sudden rush of water onto an area of land that is normally dry.

flood: when water covers an area that is usually dry, an event caused by rain, a collapsed dam, or rising sea levels.

fuel: a material used to produce heat or power by burning.

fungi: mold, mildew, rust, and mushrooms. Plural of fungus.

geography: the features of a place, such as mountains and rivers.

geyser: a hot spring under pressure that shoots boiling water or steam into the air.

glacier: a huge mass of ice and snow.

ground fire: a wildfire that burns buried vegetation.

habitat: the natural area where a plant or animal lives.

hurricane: a powerful storm with winds of at least 74 miles per hour.

igneous rock: rock that forms from cooling magma.

ignite: to burst into flames.

irrigation: the watering of land, often for crops.

lapilli: small fragments of lava resulting from a volcanic eruption.

lava: magma that has risen to the surface of the earth.

lava dome volcano: a dome-shaped volcano that forms when lava breaks through the crust and mounds up.

lava flow: a mass of flowing or solidified lava.

livestock: animals raised for food and other uses.

magma: molten rock within the layer of earth just below the earth's crust.

mantle: the layer of the earth between the crust and core.

meteorologist: a person who studies the science of weather and climate.

minerals: nutrients found in rocks and soil that keep plants and animals healthy and growing.

mold: a furry growth.

molten: made liquid by heat.

moment magnitude scale: a scale that scientists use to measure an earthquake's size and strength.

# NATURAL DISASTERS!

natural disaster: a natural event that can cause tremendous destruction to life and property.

nutrients: substances in food, water, and soil that living things need to live and grow.

organism: a living thing, such as an animal or a plant.

Pangaea: a supercontinent that existed about 300 million years ago. It contained all the land on the earth.

precipitation: fresh water that falls from clouds in the form of rain, ice, snow, hail, mist, or sleet.

preserve: to protect something so that it stays in its original state.

pressure: a force that pushes on an object.

pyroclastic flow: the current of lava and dirt that spreads out along the ground from a volcano after an eruption.

retardant: a material that slows or stops the spread of fire.

Richter scale: a scale that was used to measure the strength of an earthquake.

rotate: to turn around a fixed point.

rubble: broken fragments.

Santa Ana winds: strong, dry winds that start inland and blow toward the coast.

seismic wave: the wave of energy that travels outward from an earthquake.

seismometer: an instrument used to detect and record movement and vibration in the earth or other objects.

shaft: a short rod that allows something to spin.

shield volcano: a volcano formed from the flow of runny, non-explosive lava.

storm surge: high sea levels that can occur after a big storm, such as a hurricane.

stratovolcano: a classic cone-shaped volcano with alternating layers of lava flows and more explosive volcanic deposits.

surface fire: a wildfire that occurs on the surface of the ground, burning low-lying vegetation.

surface wave: a seismic wave that travels on the surface of the earth.

tectonic plates: large sections of the earth's crust that move on top of the hot, melted layer below.

thermal imaging: the technique of using the heat given off by an object to produce an image of it or to locate it.

topsoil: the upper layer of soil.

tornado: a swirling vortex of wind in a funnel shape that extends toward the earth from a large storm system.

tropical: having to do with the area near the equator.

tropical storm: a very strong storm that forms in the tropics.

tsunami: an enormous wave formed by a disturbance under the water, such as an earthquake or a volcano.

vent: an opening in the earth's crust.

volcano: a mountain formed by magma or ash forcing its way from deep inside the earth to the surface.

volcanologist: a scientist who studies volcanoes.

water cycle: the natural recycling of water through evaporation, condensation, precipitation, and collection.

waterspout: a tornado that occurs over water.

wildfire: a fire that spreads quickly, usually across a large area of land.

withstand: to survive.

# METRIC CONVERSIONS

Use this chart to find the metric equivalents to the English measurements in this book. If you need to know a half measurement, divide by two. If you need to know twice the measurement, multiply by two. How do you find a quarter measurement? How do you find three times the measurement?

| English | Metric |
| --- | --- |
| 1 inch | 2.5 centimeters |
| 1 foot | 30.5 centimeters |
| 1 yard | 0.9 meter |
| 1 mile | 1.6 kilometers |
| 1 pound | 0.5 kilogram |
| 1 teaspoon | 5 milliliters |
| 1 tablespoon | 15 milliliters |
| 1 cup | 237 milliliters |

# BOOKS

Challoner, Jack. *DK Eyewitness Books: Hurricane & Tornado: Encounter Nature's Most Extreme Weather Phenomena from Turbulent Twisters to Fierce Tropical Cyclones*. DK Children, 2014.

Watts, Clair and Trevor Day. *DK Eyewitness Books: Natural Disasters: Confront the Awesome Power of Nature from Earthquakes and Tsunamis to Hurricanes*. DK Children, 2015.

Galat, Joan Marie. *Erupt! 100 Fun Facts About Volcanoes*. National Geographic Partners, Inc., 2017.

Nargi, Lela. *Absolute Expert: Volcanoes*. National Geographic Kids, 2018.

Reilly, Kathleen M. *Fault Lines and Tectonic Plates: Discover What Happens When the Earth's Crust Moves*. Nomad Press, 2017.

Spilsbury, Louise and Richard. *Top 10 Worst Volcanic Eruptions*. Powerkids, 2017.

## WEBSITES

**National Geographic – Natural Disasters**
video.nationalgeographic.com/video/environment/natural-disaster

**WatchKnowLearn.org – videos about natural disasters, some feature-length**
watchknowlearn.org/Category.aspx?CategoryID=13805

**Ready.gov – website on disaster preparedness for kids:** ready.gov/kids/know-the-facts

**BrainPop – animated videos on different natural disasters**
brainpop.com/science/earthsystem/naturaldisasters

## ESSENTIAL QUESTIONS

**Introduction:** What kinds of natural disasters are common where you live?

**Chapter 1:** What are some dangers of earthquakes?

**Chapter 2:** How do volcanoes form?

**Chapter 3:** Why are rivers important?

**Chapter 4:** What are some ways that wildfires can start?

**Chapter 5:** Why are hurricanes important to the health of the planet?

## QR CODE GLOSSARY

**Page 4:** youtube.com/watch?v=11pjSTnl99Q

**Page 14:** earthquake.usgs.gov/earthquakes/search

**Page 26:** aeon.co/videos/from-eruption-to-obliteration-
the-sights-and-sounds-of-48-fateful-hours-in-pompeii

**Page 33:** earthobservatory.nasa.gov/world-of-change/StHelens

**Page 43:** droughtmonitor.unl.edu

**Page 51:** greenmatters.com/home/2018/01/04/ML8rn/
engineers-have-developed-a-system-to-make-houses-float-during-flooding

**Page 55:** nifc.gov/fireInfo/nfn.htm

**Page 57:** youtube.com/watch?v=9EzcA3KvEsY

**Page 58:** youtube.com/watch?v=yh_l4ZVNeU8

**Page 61:** fsapps.nwcg.gov/afm

**Page 61:** worldview.earthdata.nasa.gov

**Page 71:** youtube.com/watch?v=LlXVikDkyTg